Copyright © 2021, 2024 by Uschi Nagel
www.uschinagel.com
The moral right of the author has been asserted.

All rights reserved.
No part of this publication may be reproduced, stored in a retrieval system, or transmitted, in any form or by any means, without the prior permission of the publisher, not be otherwise circulated in any form of binding or cover than that in which it is published and without a similar condition including this condition being imposed on the subsequent purchaser.

Contributing Editor: Katie Soy
www.katiesoy.com

Illustrator: Robyn Bromham
www.facebook.com/robspetportraits

Print and distribution: IngramSpark

Published 2024.
First edition published 2021. Second edition 2024

ISBN 978-0-6454475-2-1

For Sunny

2007 – 2021

and Turbo

2009 – 2023

A Lifetime of Love

Content

About Grief

What to expect

Common Grief Responses

Looking after yourself (How to be gentle with your grief responses)

Hold a memorial or funeral for your pet

Watch out for unhelpful thoughts

Adjusting to a new Normal without your companion

Supporting your grieving Child

When Hope is not enough (Dealing with the Trauma of Euthanasia)

How to comfort the surviving pet

When is it time for another pet?

How to support a grieving friend

Dear Friend,

What if you turned inward to the grief of losing your beloved pet? Instead of pushing feelings of loss aside to move on, what would happen if you honored this tragic loss with reverence and self-compassion?

Honoring your pet helps you heal and keeps their spirit alive. Understand and treasure the deep connection between a pet and their human.

Many of us refuse to honor grief when our loved ones pass in a society that chooses to rush the process of loss, and look away. This is even more common when our pets pass on.

If your best friend lost a pet companion of many years, a true friend really, would you minimize the importance of their feelings? You probably wouldn't say they should move on quickly. Or that the loss was "just a pet."

Let me ask you, Sweet Soul, why utter those words to yourself?

My hope for you is to feel acknowledged and supported in the emotional pain of losing your pet. Your pain is valid and the grief for your pet is real. Your friendship with your pet is real. The relationship, love, experiences, and support were all real.

What if grieving was honoring the life your pet lived?

Rushing this process, avoiding it, or minimizing the experience does nothing to respect the memory I know you deeply wish to preserve.

Allow yourself to feel these emotions, because they are neither good nor bad, they just are.

Most importantly, be kind and gentle with your pain, carry it softly like a baby bird.

May you feel comforted and supported on your journey from Loss to Love.

Uschi Nagel

Until one has loved an animal, a part of one's soul remains unawakened.

Anatole France

We all feel it.

The bond with our pet is unique and strong.

Some say it is because the Love from an animal
is unconditional.

You treasure the precious life experiences you've shared
with friends and family.
Adventures with your beloved pet
are no different.

After all, they often experience the
ordinary and extraordinary moments of life with us
before other people do.

They're there in times of tragedy,
and in times of joy.

For birthdays.

For promotions.

For life milestones.

For loss. And birth.

And rainstorms. And days with the flu.

They are by our side for the moments that make up life.

About Grief

Grief is normal and a healthy response to a major loss. Grief can begin before the anticipated loss when your pet is diagnosed with a terminal illness.

Around significant events like anniversaries or holidays, we can fall back into acute grief, which is a normal part of the grieving process. This does not represent a failure.

If a friend was processing the loss of a loved one, and experienced more grief during a holiday, would you view that as a failure to cope? Of course not. You would compassionately understand the trigger.

Can you do the same with yourself and your pet?

It can get complicated when we experience "traumatic" grief, which occurs when grief becomes chronic, disabling, and more intense.
That is when it might be helpful to seek professional support.

Please remember:

Asking for support is an act of courage.

*Find comfort in knowing
you gave a little innocent soul
a wonderful life,
and this little cat knew kindness
and Love for all that time.*

What to expect

While our grief tends to have a forward trajectory and people might believe that time heals all wounds, it does take a conscious amount of effort and work.
Grief can be triggered anytime and it is not unusual for grief to be felt over a long period of time.
The process of grief is unique and certainly not linear, but there are steps you can take when dealing with a loss:

Acknowledging and Accepting the Loss
Loss is painful. The reality of our pet not coming back may feel unbearable. You have permission to acknowledge the significance of the death and the pain that comes with it.

Processing the Pain of our Loss
We can feel grief psychologically as well as physically. It is normal to experience different reactions when grieving. There is no need to hide or bury your grief. It is appropriate and deserves expression.

What to expect

Honoring Life and Loss
It is easy and common to minimize grief related to pet loss. This slows down the grief process and can even cause more pain.
Honor the life and shared experiences with your pet by not pushing your feelings aside.

Being Gentle with Yourself After Loss
Treat yourself with kindness while you grieve. Let go of any expectations about your grief entirely. They are not helpful. Know that we grieve as who we are. If we usually show emotions, we most likely will show them now, or if we don't, we probably won't. And that's OK.

Focus on your basic everyday needs. This will help you deal with grief better physically and emotionally.

Common Grief Responses

Emotional
- Sadness
- Guilt
- Anger
- Anxiety
- Fatigue
- Feeling lonely
- Feeling overwhelmed
- Feeling numb
- Feeling helpless / powerless

Physical reactions
- Nausea
- Shock
- Pain in the stomach area
- Chest tightness
- Dry mouth
- Shortness of breath
- Difficulty sleeping
- Loss of appetite
- Restlessness
- Poor Concentration

*It's a fearful thing to love
what death can touch*

Yehuda Halevi

Looking after yourself

How to be gentle with your grief responses

Be patient and be kind to yourself;
rest when you need to.

Connect with nature and go for walks or a bike ride.

Listen to music or read a book.

Light a candle in remembrance.

Surround yourself with people who can support you.

Call and talk to a trusted friend.

Hold a memorial or funeral for your pet.

We have birthday parties, funerals, and weddings for a reason. All these events have something in common.

Birthdays occur whether we celebrate or not.

Death happens without a celebration of life.

People commit to one another without a ceremony.

However, rituals can be useful in acknowledging and processing your loss. They help us emotionally engage with life milestones.

There is comfort in gathering with people who also loved your pet, sharing stories, crying together, and realizing that the pain we feel reflects our care and connection.

There is joy in celebrating special moments or adventures you have experienced with your pet.

A creative outlet like writing or making memorabilia for your pet can help with making sense of the loss.

Remember, there is no timeline for grief.
It takes as long as it takes.

Try not to grieve as others might expect of you. Your reaction to loss is unique and yours alone.

However, if your feelings are persistent and distressing, please reach out and get professional support.

And just when you think you are starting to adjust, reality hits.

He is gone forever.

Watch out for unhelpful thoughts

Grief can be prolonged by having thoughts of regret and doubt, creating even more pain and sorrow.
Not only are you mourning the loss of your companion, but you might also ruminate about the mistakes you might have made, including the inability to "just move on".

"Shouldn't I be over this by now?"
"Life isn't fair"
"If only I had done something different"
"It's all my fault"
"It was only a dog/cat"

It might seem like your head and heart are arguing, not agreeing. Thoughts like these can be confusing.
They keep us stuck, they minimize our loss and delay our healing journey.

If a child processes something deeply emotional, would you dismiss their feelings? Would you berate them? No.

So why treat yourself this way during such a painful moment of losing your pet?

It is okay to accept all your feelings and reactions to your loss.

Give yourself permission to feel all the feelings that arise with grace and kindness.

Grieving isn't about letting go or moving on, but instead learning to live without your pet while also carrying them in your heart.

How do I part this sea of tears while diving deeply into sorrow?

How do I embrace the heartbreak
and find the joy contained in happy memories?
How can I tell where you are and how you may be?
When all I know is, I miss you so.

The quiet and empty house

**Adjusting to a new Normal
without your Companion**

When our pet dies,
we do not only lose their physical presence.
There may be other losses, like the loss of a
shared life, our daily routine,
waking up with our pet, feeding the pet,
going for a walk
or coming home after work to be greeted.

And all of the ordinary life adventures
experienced together.

It's not just about losing a pet.

You lost a friend.

Be gentle with yourself as it takes time
to adjust to your new surroundings
and to develop a new routine.

How do I help my child when a pet dies?

This is a common worry for parents. Often the first experience of death for a child involves the death of a pet.

The bond between a child and a pet can be very strong. For a child, a pet brings a responsibility of care, while at the same time offering precious and joyous moments.

Children tend to be extremely affectionate with their pet since they keep them company and can become a symbol of emotional security in an unsure world.
Pets give a sense of complete acceptance and loyalty. They stay close and supportive during hard times.

When a family pet dies, the child can grieve deeply for it. Parents are often concerned about the effect the loss has on the child.

Supporting your grieving child

Allow the child to grieve and be heard.

Reassure them that their feelings are okay, and provide opportunities to express them.

Let them ask questions and answer truthfully (and age appropriately).

Keep their usual schedules and routines.

Hug them, hold them, and show them Love.
This will reassure them that they are safe.

Explain that they are not responsible for the death.

Include them in the family's grieving process and let them participate in any grieving rituals.

Choose appropriate mementos like photos for a memory box or the animal's collar.

You were my favorite "hello",

but my hardest "goodbye".

When Hope is not enough

Although our hope is for our animal companions to live a long, healthy life and pass peacefully curled up in their sleep, illness or injury may instead be cutting short the time we expect to have with them. And at times we are faced with the heartbreaking decision of helping them pass when they are suffering.

Thinking about taking your pet to the vet for her final goodbye might be one of the most difficult things you ever have to do. Saying goodbye and the subsequent loss can be tremendously painful and soul-crushing.

Euthanasia can be one of the most traumatic parts of pet loss, and the agonizing decision can seem overwhelming.
It can leave us with immense regret and incredible guilt.

After your pet has died, you may wonder if a different treatment, another intervention, even another day might have changed the outcome.

These feelings of doubt, self-blame and regret are understandable. Yet, please know that you are not responsible for the loss of your pet.
It is the illness or event that took your pet's life.

It can be devastating to let a companion animal go, and it can be a challenge to ease feelings of emptiness and pain.

Therefore, please recognize when it would be helpful to reach out to a trusted health professional for support!

The hardest thing to do is to take away their pain, and make it ours.

When walking the valley of Grief,
recognize that
the deepest time of sadness
also holds the greatest Love.

How to comfort the surviving pet?

The loss of a pet is a difficult time for your whole family. Animals are capable of experiencing loss and grief, and they can mourn for their companion in similar ways we do.
It might be difficult to support your pet when you are grieving yourself, but extending comfort to your surviving pet may bring ease and healing to everyone.
Pets tend to react to the absence in a way that indicates they miss their friend. This might be enhanced by the emotional state of their humans.

Cats can be sensitive to these emotions, while dogs might feel uncertain about their new role in the family. Dogs might also struggle to adjust to change and will miss canine play time and interaction with their companion.
Dogs are generally focused on their immediate family and other pets within the family unit. Hence, losing a family member can create a void in their lives and requires extra support to deal with the loss.

What are the signs?

- Withdrawal, less active.
- Sad or moody.
- Sleeps more than usual.
- Demanding more attention than usual.
- Change in appetite.
- Searching for the other pet.
- Sleeping in the deceased's spot.
- Hiding or avoiding family members.
- Showing signs of separation anxiety like crying or barking when you leave.
- Destructive behavior like scratching furniture or not using the litter box properly.

Your pet has lost so much, a relative, a friend, an ally, a play mate.

What can you do to help?

- What does your pet need? Be available when they need you, but give them space when they want it.

- May be your withdrawn dog enjoys going for a longer walk or your cat likes to have more play time with their favorite toy.

- At times their behavior might get reinforced by your attention. Find the balance between rewarding unwanted behavior and consoling them.

- Remember that pets who positively navigate their way through the grief journey usually improve progressively over time.

- However, if your pet does not improve or starts to display health issues like vomiting or weight loss, it might be advisable to consult your veterinarian.

When is it time for another pet?

There is no wrong or right way to consider this; it is a very personal decision.

Right after your loss, it might be helpful to defer this decision when your perspective might most likely be clouded by grief.

Introducing another pet too soon might also add more stress to an already demanding situation.

It is okay to embrace the feeling of loss, connect with what matters every day, and treat yourself with kindness and compassion.

It is okay to let your soul heal and take time to process and honor the pet you have lost.

We all have the capacity to love deeply and treasure the contributions pets offer to us.

This does not end with their death, which has left such a painful void in our hearts.

Nothing can replace the wonderful experiences you had with your precious companion. How could it ever be?

Yet, the capacity to love an animal never disappears.

What if there was a chance that at some point, you would sense a gentle wish to open your home and heart to another companion?

What if there was a possibility that another furry companion could transform the pain of loss into growth that Love alone can offer?

A dog is the only thing on earth that loves you more than he loves himself.

Josh Billing

How to support a grieving friend

Listen without judgement

Sharing the story of what happened and the timeline leading up to the loss can help make sense of this painful experience for your friend and can be most healing.

Listening deeply is a special gift you can give and will be well received.

Provide support

Especially in the early stages of grief, your friend might be tired and can't think clearly.

Offering practical support like going shopping or cleaning the house might be helpful.

Simply ask: "What can I do to help you right now?"

Share memories

Talking about the beloved pet's life and all the good memories can bring comfort and help the process of loss. Offer to join in or organize a celebration of life for your friend's pet.

Talk

Often, we do not know what to say to someone who is grieving. It's okay to say that we do not know what to say and that we are very sorry for their loss. Ask them what they need and how you can help.

Try not to minimize the loss by saying things like "Fluffy had a good life", or "at least she is not in pain anymore". The grieving person might feel they are being denied the pain and it might hinder their healing.

Encourage your friend to seek professional support when their distress is affecting their life negatively.

Grief never ends,
but it changes.

It's a passage,
not a place to stay.

Grief is not a sign of weakness,
nor a lack of faith.

It's the price of Love.

Elizabeth I

Not the End

... until we meet again

Author

Uschi Nagel is a qualified Counsellor and undercover crazy cat lady with a passion for the wellbeing of all four-legged fur friends and their humans.

Many people experience the tragic passing of an animal companion and commonly find themselves struggling to cope with what has happened. Uschi understands the complexity of dealing with this challenge and focuses on supporting people after losing a beloved pet.

After the sudden death of her dog Sunny, Uschi wrote her first book "From Loss to Love", which gives comfort and practical support to assist on the painful journey after pet loss. The extended second edition of the book was published a few months after the death of her beloved cat Turbo.

Uschi lives in Australia with her family and a new puppy. She loves the beach and adores Batman.

You can find her on the web at www.uschinagel.com

References

Aid, T. (2016). Grief psychoeducation. Therapist Aid. https://www.therapistaid.com/therapy-guide/grief-psychoeducation-guide

About grief. (n.d.). https://www.grief.org.au/ga/Content/Information-Sheets/About-Grief.aspx?WebsiteKey=9af4e8a8-8d75-4439-b2f8-b00b7b41ff21

Dobias, P. (2023, May 18). When sadness and love come together. Dr. Dobias Natural Healing. https://peterdobias.com/blogs/blog/when-sadness-and-love-come-together

Fine, A. H. (Ed.). (2015). Handbook on animal-assisted therapy: Foundations and guidelines for animal-assisted interventions (4th ed.). Elsevier Academic Press.

Harvard Health. (2017, June 22). Coping with the loss of a pet. https://www.health.harvard.edu/blog/11876-2017062211876

Hayes, S. (2018). From Loss to Love. Psychology Today. https://www.psychologytoday.com/au/articles/201806/loss-love

Wall, D. (2021). Bereavement. ABCT – Association for Behavioral and Cognitive Therapies. https://www.abct.org/fact-sheets/bereavement/

Wolfelt, Alan D. (2004). The Understanding Your Grief Support Group Guide. Fort Collins: Companion Press, Fort Collins, USA.

www.ingramcontent.com/pod-product-compliance
Lightning Source LLC
Chambersburg PA
CBHW061800290426
44109CB00030B/2903